A NEW SONG RISES UP!

STUDY GUIDE

CARIN JAYNE CASEY

Casey, Carin Jayne. *A New Song Rises Up! Study Guide*

Copyright © 2020 by Carin Jayne Casey

Published by KWE Publishing: www.kwepub.com

ISBN (paperback): 978-1-950306-67-1 (ebook): 978-1-950306-68-8

Unless otherwise noted, scripture in this book taken from the Authorized King James Bible. (Published by the World Publishing Company, New York.) New International Version (NIV) Holy Bible, New International Version ® NIV ® Copyright © 1973, 1978, 1984, 2011 by Biblica, Inc. ® Used by permission. All rights reserved worldwide.

Casey, Carin Jayne: A New Song Rises Up! Study Guide

1. Christian Living - Social Issues 2. Christian Living - Inspirational 3. Body, Mind and Spirit - Healing - Prayers & Spiritual

NATIONAL DOMESTIC VIOLENCE HOTLINE

1-800-799-7233 or (TTY) 1-800-787-3224

INTRODUCTION

This *Study Guide* is meant to be utilized as a learning tool while you read *A New Song Rises Up!* Some of your questions found in *A New Song Rises Up!* are repeated here so that you can record your answers for convenience and some readers prefer not to write notes in their books. I believe it would be most effective if you read a chapter in the book, then work in the corresponding study guide chapter as you navigate through. It is your decision if you prefer to read the entire book first. For best results, be honest and authentic with yourself as you respond. If you currently live in an unsafe or toxic environment, you may need to ensure privacy or safekeeping of this Study Guide. If your copy is in e-book format, you will need to record your responses and notes on separate paper or a journal.

Congratulations! You are here because you have decided that you want to navigate through your challenges in a positive way while, at the same time, enjoying peace, not fear.

My desire is to help you learn from the problems you face and to become empowered, content, and at peace along your journey. That desire for your deliverance was dropped into my spirit with abounding gratitude when I had recovered from horrible and life-threatening experiences.

I came to realize that through my own dark days, there is ultimately light:

- I was not alone; the Lord was with me.
- Everything that happened, both good and bad, can be utilized as learning tools for my growth.
- As the Lord rescued me time after time my faith increased, as well as a compassion for others in those same areas.
- It was because of my valuable learning through the hard times that enabled me to share the recipe to overcome, which can be applied to any challenge in life.
- I know my unique purpose, what I was created for; as I serve the Lord and others within my calling, my life becomes complete.

This is my testimony: I was close to death in the pit of despair. But God heard my desperate cry. Now within me, I have a new song to sing, that of praise to my Awesome Deliverer.

What I want for every reader is positive, redemptive change. Regardless of any situation you may face, I hope for you to discover your secret of inner peace and joy. Find victory in Jesus!

1

PROLOGUE

This chapter began with an emotionally charged scene of my abuser proving his infidelity in our relationship by insisting that I go and witness his interactions with one of his mistresses...

Can you imagine what emotional pain or upset a victim might experience when faced with this type of scene? If so, please list some of these feelings.

What harm do you believe the abuser had hoped to accomplish by bringing these two women together?

Why did the abuser refuse to let his victim dress up and put on make-up before meeting the other woman?

What mixed feelings would you have toward the other woman? Would you be able to view her as another victim?

Have you ever experienced this type of betrayal by someone you cared about? How did you feel?

In domestic violence situations, there is usually a breaking point when the victim says, "Enough!" Have you ever been in an abusive or toxic situation and reached such a point? Can you briefly describe it?

What was your defining moment like? How did you feel after making that decision? What changed in your mindset? Were you then able to separate your emotional ties with that abuser? Ultimately, was there a sense of empowerment?

Have you ever been in an abusive or toxic relationship where the other person had convinced you it was your fault for their bad behavior? Do you now see that an abuser (anyone) is responsible for their own behavior?

Do you agree or disagree that as adults, we are each responsible for how we react badly or respond kindly to any situation?

Facing the ugly truth about someone you once cared about is hard, but important for when you face future encounters. Your eyes are open! Can you recall a terrible incident you had experienced, and now see where someone in it had orchestrated what happened? Maybe it involved lies or manipulations that you were not able to see at that time?

Can you remember a time when the enemy (your adversary, an abuser or toxic person) said or did something meant to harm you, but God turned it for your good in the aftermath?

David remembered the Lord was with him while he was a shepherd boy killing the lion and the bear with a sling shot. Remembering this brought David confidence that the Lord was with him when he faced Goliath. Do you understand how it builds your faith for future challenges to recall another time when the Lord has delivered you?

Refer to my first epiphany. Was there anything from my first epiphany that you could relate to or use as a learning tool?

Have you ever turned your back on God, believing that you were self-sufficient, only later to learn you needed Him to rescue you? What did you do? Were you hesitant to turn to Him, ashamed and thinking you had gone too far for His mercy?

Can you relate to the remorse I felt when I realized I had turned my back on the Lord, after all He had delivered me from already? Do you have similar remorse that you can confess to Him about? What happens when you humbly repent, believe in, and accept Jesus?

Was it encouraging for you when you read my testimony that despite my sinful life and turning from Him, the Lord was merciful and heard my cry for help?

Your Heavenly Father is available for you as well. The Lord forgave me, He rescued me, and through Jesus Christ, He saved me. If he did this for me, He can and will do it for you. Do you believe this?

Please meditate on the following scripture. Can you relate to it? Do you believe a new song is rising up in your life?

> He stooped down to lift me out of danger from
> the desolate pit I was in,
> out of the muddy mess I had fallen into.
> Now He's lifted me up into a firm, secure place and steadied me
> while I walk along His ascending path.
> A new song for a new day rises up in me every time I think about
> how He breaks through for me!
> Ecstatic praise pours out of my mouth until everyone hears how
> God has set me free.
> Many will see His miracles; they'll stand in awe of God
> and fall in love with Him!
> Psalm 40:2-3 (TPT) The Passion Translation (emphasis added)

Affirmation Statement:

Write an affirmation, with a corresponding scripture or reference. *(for example, from Psalm 40:2-3 noted above, "Whenever I'm in trouble, my God rescues me.")*

Gratitude Statement:

Write something you are grateful to the Lord for (recommended daily). *(for example, "I love and praise the Lord because He has set me free!")*

2

ARE YOU BELIEVING THE LIES?

In this chapter, we address the issue of child abuse in a dysfunctional family. Did you find scenes that you could resonate with? What were the similarities?

As a child, did you ever need a parent or another person in authority to stand up for you, or to rescue you, but they did not do it? How did this betrayal or failure to protect affect you?

When parents or other people in authority failed you, did you feel or tell yourself that you were not enough, or unlovable? Do you believe that about yourself now?

Did you relate to any of these lies the enemy had impressed on me? Designate when this happened. Why did you believe these lies? Are you breaking free of these lies now?

- You are not worthy.

- Your sins were so great that God will not forgive you.

- God has left you alone in this.

- What you do or don't do is of no importance to God.

Please meditate on the following scripture. What is your response?

"... He's been a murderer right from the start!
He never stood with the One who is the true Prince, for he's full of
nothing but lies—
lying is his native tongue. He is a master of deception and the
father of lies!"
John 8:44 (TPT) The Passion Translation

God's Word, which was breathed by Him, says that the enemy is a liar. Can you prayerfully and consciously free your mindset from the negative and ugly lies you had believed about yourself?

Did you experience debilitating struggles or life-threatening situations? Was part of your heartbreak because your troubles were by someone who should have loved you?

And yet, you are here now. You were not destroyed! Can you find strength in knowing God wants the best for you? Can you allow yourself to receive His best?

Through the Lord's divine intervention, you can face the truth about yourself, and those chains that have held you down can be broken. Do you believe it? Can you see that God, your Creator loves you and your loved ones even more than you do?

Have you pushed ugly stuff deep inside you? Do you realize that it is still there, affecting you in negative ways? Can you bring it to light and talk to the Lord about it? That is your first step toward overcoming!

Please meditate on the following scripture. How does it affect you? Does it change your view of yourself?

> Before I formed you in the womb, I knew you...
> Jeremiah 1:5 (NIV) New International Version

Have you ever compared your life with another person, only to find out they had terrible issues to face that you would never want? Can you agree that comparisons never bring a positive outcome?

Have you learned valuable lessons through your challenges in life? Do you see why those same struggles may have helped you to mature?

When bad stuff happens, do you wonder why? Do you ask these questions as you try to figure it out?

- Is it the evilness of this world affecting me?
- Is God allowing something to come along because it will eventually help me to mature?
- Could it be a small part in the bigger picture for good in the grand scheme of things?
- Am I being punished for my wrongdoings?

I encourage you to read and study the story of Joseph, Genesis 37 through 50. Ultimately, Joseph explained (as follows) to his brothers (who had sold him into slavery):

> You intended to harm me, but God intended it all for good.
> Genesis 50:20 (NLT) New Living Translation

Can you think of a situation in your life when someone intended your harm, but the end result (maybe years later) was for your good?

Do you believe that even while in the midst of bad stuff happening, we can rest in the knowledge that God is ultimately in control? Do you have faith that God is always loving, good, and just, even when we do not understand?

Did you ever wonder what your life purpose is? Did you think you were an accident? Have you asked God, "Who am I, and why am I here?"

Please meditate on the following scriptures. Do they help you to realize you were no accident? Do you realize that you were born with a unique purpose?

> "For I know the plans I have for you," says the Lord.
> "They are plans for good and not for disaster, to give you
> a future and a hope."
> Jeremiah 29:11 (NLT) New Living Translation

> You saw me before I was born. Every day of my life
> was recorded in your book.
> Every moment was laid out before a single day had passed.
> Psalm 139:16 (NLT) New Living Translation

Can you think of a time when God *used* what the enemy meant for harm, and made it work for good in your situation? Were you grateful? Can you write it down and recall that incident for the next time the enemy attacks?

Please meditate on the following scripture. Does it give you confidence and hope for the future? What is the requirement we must fulfill?

> And we know that God causes everything to work together for the
> good of those who love God and are called
> according to his purpose for them.
> Romans 8:28 (NLT) New Living Translation

Affirmation Statement:

Write an affirmation, with a corresponding scripture or reference. *(for example, from Ephesians 2:10 (NLT), "I am God's Workmanship.")*

Gratitude Statement:

Write something you are grateful to the Lord for (recommended daily).

3

ARE YOU INVISIBLE?

In this chapter, we talk about instances where a person may be treated as though they were invisible. Have you ever experienced this? Did it hurt your feelings?

Were you treated as if you were invisible by someone you respected during your pre-adult years? Did it promote your sense of isolation or negative feelings about yourself? Were those feelings lasting?

Please meditate on the following scripture. Do you find comfort in what Jesus says to you now? Jesus said:

> A thief has only one thing in mind—
> he wants to steal, slaughter, and destroy.
> But I have come to give you everything in abundance,
> more than you expect—
> life in its fullness until you overflow!

John 10:10 (TPT) The Passion Translation

Do you have any residual ugly stuff that continues to cause you pain inside? Have you decided to turn to God for help?

In what ways can you get help to become the best person or parent feasible, and to build a solid foundation for a healthy and loving legacy?

Does a pity-party, whether by yourself or with listeners, ultimately make your situation better or worse?

To become victim to abuse is terrible. Do you agree that these options would be worse?

- Not to learn lessons from past experiences;
- To continue in relationships where abuse exists;
- To withhold sharing your testimony with others about how the Lord scooped you out of a horrible pit; and
- To be unable or unwilling to present the world with a better plan than a legacy of abuse.

In my testimony, I shared instances of physical abuse, and of betrayal. Can you relate to either? Both? Which left the most lasting effects on you? Why?

Were you ever in the arena of favoritism? How did that feel? Were there lasting affects? Have you ever been guilty of showing favoritism?

Was the story about Abraham's family history (Genesis 27-37) and the on-going favoritism and jealousy helpful for you?

Do you believe a legacy of favoritism has continued among your loved ones? What can you do?

Please meditate on the following scripture. Does it help you to beware of evil temptations that surround you daily?

Be well balanced and always alert, because your enemy, the devil,
roams around incessantly, like a roaring lion
looking for its prey to devour.
1 Peter 5:8 (TPT) The Passion Translation

Please answer these questions relating to any type of pre-adult physical, verbal, or other abuses you may have experienced:

- Were you less likely to come into adulthood with confidence and high self-esteem?
- Did you tend to view yourself as not enough, unworthy, and unloved?
- How did your emotions run? Angry, bitter, depressed, or sad?
- Did you lack trust in others?
- Did you pattern your behavior after those who have been abusive to you?
- Because of the various levels of dissociation in your past, did you find yourself unable to adequately express your emotions?

Correspondingly, did you see how your behavior and feelings may have caused negative effects within your normal life cycles? For instance:

Education

Career path

Family, Friends, and Intimate partner

Health

Most importantly, did you model how you viewed God after that parent or person who held power and authority over you?

- Did you view the Lord as an unpredictable mixture of love and brutality?
- Were you invisible to Him?
- Did you view God as authoritarian to the point you did the maximum good works and rituals of prayers in hopes for Him to dole out love in your direction?
- Did you become a workaholic, with no sense of satisfaction?
- Were you less likely to love, trust, and rely upon the Lord in faith?
- Did you automatically feel rejected by Him, and thus never turn to Him at all?

- Because you did not feel worthy for God's love, maybe you angrily rejected Him?

Please comment on each aspect of the recipe to overcome. Have you completed your steps?

1. Turn to God

Do you believe that turning to God is the first and most important step you will ever take?

Please meditate on the following scriptures. What do they tell you?

For God so loved the world that he gave his one and only Son, that
whoever believes in him shall not perish
but have eternal life.
John 3:16 (NIV) New International Version

Jesus said: I am the way and the truth and the life.
No one comes to the Father
except through me.
John 14:6 (NIV) New International Version)

Please read and study the following scriptures about salvation, and write one of them down:

Romans 10:9-10 and 1 John 1:9

2. Safely Leave your Dangerous Environment

This step is very dangerous *and* necessary. Where can you get expert assistance? What are your resources? Who can help in devising an escape plan?

Emergency, dial "911"

The National Domestic Violence Hotline 1-800- 799- 7233 (SAFE)

Have you remained in an abusive or toxic environment because you thought you had no choice?

Please meditate on the following statements. How do they resonate with you?

Please know the Lord did not mean for you to remain in a habitually toxic environment.

You might say, "I have to stay in it, it's my _____." (fill in the blank: boss, in-laws, church member, etc.). But it doesn't matter who that habitually mean-spirited person is. They have caused their presence around you to become a toxic environment!

Do you have relationships with people who will build you up? Will they encourage you? Are they loving, kind, and speak good things? List their first names.

If you have not yet surrounded yourself with people such as these, can you pursue friendships with people with these qualities? List their first names.

3. Have Faith and Believe

Have you turned to Jesus for your salvation? Please share your story of when you turned to God and accepted Jesus as your Lord and Savior.

Please read and study Jeremiah 31:3 and Isaiah 41:10. Write one of them below.

In a few short sentences, please share your testimony.

Without Jesus, this is how I viewed myself:

With Jesus, this is who I am:

4. Gratitude

What has the Lord done for you and what storms has He rescued you from that you are thankful for?

Please read and study Philippians 4:4 and 1 Thessalonians 5:16-18 and write one of them down.

Do you agree or disagree that it's impossible to have a pity-party while being thankful?

5. Forgiveness

We forgive ourselves, the abusers in our lives, and we forgive those who remained indifferent to our need for help. Can you see how forgiveness is for your own soul's sake?

Which is hardest to do—forgiving yourself, your offenders, or those who were indifferent to your needs? Why? How can you get past it?

Is there anyone you need to forgive today? What do you need to do?

Please read and study: 1 Peter 5:7 and Matthew 6: 14-15 and write one of them down.

Can you resonate with the recipe to overcome? Which has been your most difficult step to accomplish?

How are you doing with your steps toward overcoming?

Affirmation Statement:

Write an affirmation, with a corresponding scripture or reference.

Gratitude Statement:

Write something you are grateful to the Lord for (recommended daily).

4

WILL THE OFFENSES STOP?

In this chapter, we explore the pattern of offenses that have happened during seasons in our lives to see what we can learn for the future.

Could you relate to the description I gave about myself as "a naïve, vulnerable little rug"?

What are the lessons you have learned from that experience?

Was there a period of promiscuity or other self-devaluating incidents in your timeline? Did you feel as if you had a target drawn on you for attracting mean or negative people?

Did you push nice, stable, and supporting people away from you?

Please ask yourself these questions as your own insightful self-evaluation:

- Was I needy? Am I needy now?
- Was I reckless in the choices I made? Am I reckless now?
- Did I allow myself to be a rug to others?
- Am I a rug for people now?

Please meditate on the following statements. Can you see how negative it is for you to say and believe these statements?

"It wasn't my fault, I was a victim." Bringing it forward, "It's not my fault, I am a victim."

Do you practice negative self-talk? Can you see how destructive it is for you to belittle yourself and to have self-loathing because you allowed someone to use and abuse you? Can you forgive yourself and replace the negative self-talk to positive, affirming and building statements?

When you have true remorse or guilt for something you thought, said, or did, which of these is the best course of action to deal with that guilt?

- Should you carry it with you for the rest of your life?
- Can you ask the Lord to forgive you?
- Can you repent repeatedly and still mentally beat yourself up?
- How many times do you need to take that guilt in repentance to the Lord for His forgiveness?

Please meditate on the following scriptures. What message did you receive from them?

"... For I will forgive their wickedness and will remember their
sins no more."
Jeremiah 31:34 (NIV) New International Version

"Forget the former things; do not dwell on the past.
See, I am doing a new thing!
Now it springs up; do you not perceive it?
I am making a way in the wilderness
and streams in the wasteland..."
Isaiah 43:18-19 (NIV) New International Version

Do you believe that God heard you the first time you came to Him in humble repentance? Knowing that He knew your heart and forgave you, why would you remind Him and yourself of what has been forgiven?

Does it matter what other people think? Do their opinions matter?

Some people will choose to judge you harshly, maybe for a long time. Is that their problem or yours?

Have you allowed another person's critical outlook to cause you to act as a people-pleaser? Have you let their opinion bring your own sense of self-worth down?

Have you been guilty of judging, criticizing, or gossiping about another person? How can you remedy that?

Please meditate on the following scripture. How does it affect your outlook of this temporary life on earth verses life forever with Jesus?

"...And everything I've taught you is so that the peace which is in me will be in you and will give you great confidence as you rest in me. For in this unbelieving world you will experience trouble and sorrows, but you must be courageous, for I have conquered the world!"
John 16:33 (TPT) The Passion Translation

Did you accept Jesus? Do you believe that He is with you through your every struggle?

Please read and study Psalm 55:22. Can you cast your cares on the Lord? What is the promise received when you give Him your burdens?

Do you believe that although there may be hard times to endure, He always ultimately works it out for good for those who love Him?

. . .

Was it encouraging to read in *A New Song Rises Up* about how the Apostle Paul had been before he converted to Christianity? If God could forgive him, a persecutor of Christians, is there hope that He will forgive you?

Please read and study 1 Thessalonians 5:16-18. What was the Apostle Paul's secret to remaining content, regardless of what happened around him?

Please read and study Psalm 61:1-4. Who do you call when trouble comes and tries to overwhelm you?

Affirmation Statement:

Write an affirmation, with a corresponding scripture or reference.

Gratitude Statement:

Write something you are grateful to the Lord for (recommended daily).

5

WHAT CAN YOU DO ABOUT TOXIC PEOPLE?

Toxic people, do you know any? Here in this chapter, we look at some of the characteristics that an abuser or toxic person may possess and consider whether we have such a person within our circle of influence.

Please meditate on the following statement. Do you agree? If you agree, how much easier is it for you NOT to become 'the hero' in the future?

Whenever a person presents you as their only possible hope, deliverer, or hero in their situation, most likely they already have in mind the next hero if you won't comply (they have a plan B).

How do you feel once you are away from your potentially toxic person? Relieved? Upset? Angry? Drained? Be sure it is the person bringing that feeling to you, and not something else! I recall deciding not to visit a certain friend because I always left her presence feeling nervous. Later I realized that we would drink huge glasses of tea upon each visit, something I do not normally do. Much later I realized that it was the caffeine in the tea, not her, that made me nervous!

Please review the recipe to overcome. If you know someone who has been habitually toxic, what steps can you take? Can you decide not to let yourself be exposed to that toxic person?

If you decide to allow yourself to go again into a known toxic environment, please think on the following questions and reconsider that decision.

- How do you plan to respond to the toxicity? Would it make a difference?
- Will you say or do nothing, essentially indicating agreement or encouragement to bad behavior?
- Do you anticipate having negative or hurt feelings as a result of the encounter?
- Would you practice tough love? What would that look like?
- Would others within that group be with you or against you if you try to evoke change?
- Do you expect a different response than what you've been receiving?
- Is there reason to expect a positive outcome?

What are some similarities and differences of an environment with a habitually toxic person compared to a domestic violence environment?

Please meditate on the following statement. What is your response?
"You are *not* required to remain in a habitually toxic or abusive situation no matter who it is."

If a person does not care about you, even hates you, it feels very personal, doesn't it? Can you understand that it's about the condition of their heart, and it's not about you?

Would you be able to walk away from that habitual toxic person or group praying to the Lord, as Jesus did during His crucifixion, "Father, forgive them, for they know not what they do"?

Please read and study Proverbs 22:24-25; James 3:16; 1 Corinthians 15:33; Proverbs 6:16-19; and 2 Corinthians 6:14. What is the character of the people who you are surrounding yourself with? Are they emanating light or darkness into your personal space? What is influencing you?

Are you spending your time with like-minded believers who are positive, loving, and kind, who will encourage you and lift you up, not try to tear you down?

Affirmation Statement:

Write an affirmation, with a corresponding scripture or reference.

Gratitude Statement:

Write something you are grateful to the Lord for (recommended daily).

6

HOW CAN YOU HEAL FROM THE PAIN?

In this chapter, we talk about healing from emotional and physical pain.

Emotional Pain

Have you suffered from emotional pain due to the loss of a loved one?

Was it through betrayal, death, or other reasons?

Are you hurting now? What is bothering you the most? Have you talked to the Lord about it?

Do you believe that your season of grieving has lasted too long?

Can you ask others to pray for you? Is there a pastor who can console you about it?

Please read and study 1 Thessalonians 4:13-15. If you suffer from the death of a loved one, does this passage give you comfort?

Did the story about King David and God's plan for restoration in 1 Samuel 30 give you hope? In Verse 6, "David found strength in the Lord his God." Can you turn to God for your strength?

Our emotional pain is often filled with a mixture of loss, regret, and destroyed dreams. In the story of King David and Bathsheba, found in 2 Samuel: 11-12, there is sorrow with mourning and sin with consequence. Yet, there is forgiveness and hope for a good future. Was there anything in this story that you could resonate with and find hope?

Please read and study Isaiah 61:1-3. Here we see that the Spirit of the Lord seeks to heal the brokenhearted, to comfort all who mourn, to trade in our ashes for beauty, and to exchange our mourning for the oil of joy. Do you find hope and comfort from this scripture?

Please meditate on the following scripture. How does it bring promise that Jesus will comfort those who mourn? But what is your part in it? Do you believe and have faith that He keeps His promises?

Jesus said: Blessed are those who mourn,
for they will be comforted.
Matthew 5:4 (NIV) New International Version

Physical Pain

Have you had an experience that brought you lasting physical pain?
Maybe you were in an accident, or had a physical defect to deal
with?

Was there a process of stages in your recovery to contend with? Are
you in physical pain now?

What does it take to maintain a positive attitude of hope
throughout your recovery?

What is the focus of your patient faith: in yourself, in your doctor's
expertise, or in the Lord?

Does consistent gratitude toward the Lord play a part in your
healing process?

Please meditate on the following scripture and find at least two
more scriptures for healing to study. I recommend you write down
one and memorize it.

> Heal me, O Lord, and I shall be healed;
> Save me, and I shall be saved,
> For You *are* my praise.
> Jeremiah 17:14 (NKJV) New King James Version

Did you know that you could also put your favorite scripture to a tune and sing it out loud? While I sing Jeremiah 17:14, I am praying for forgiveness, healing, and salvation; singing praise to Him; and demonstrating my faith in Him. Can you do the same with a healing scripture?

Do you think Jesus can understand our suffering? What are some of the emotional and physical pains Jesus experienced while on earth?

Please meditate on the following scripture and detail what message you find in it for you.

> All praises belong to the God and Father of our Lord Jesus Christ.
> For He is the Father of tender mercy and the God of endless
> comfort. He always comes alongside us to comfort us
> in every suffering so that we can come
> alongside those who are in any painful trial.
> We can bring them this same comfort that
> God has poured out upon us.
> 2 Corinthians 1:3-4 (TPT) The Passion Translation
> (emphasis added)

Affirmation Statement:

Write an affirmation, with a corresponding scripture or reference.

Gratitude Statement:

Write something you are grateful to the Lord for (recommended daily).

7

DOES SIN APPLY TO YOU?

In this chapter, we take on the gift of conviction; we dare to open our eyes to see within ourselves if there is any sin we need to deal with. We examine ourselves knowing that we can repent, walk away from that sinful life-style, and be cleansed.

Do you know there are things you are doing that are not quite right? Are you playing a game, hoping you will get by with it? Do you want to get better?

Can you agree with me that facing hard truths may not be pleasant at the time, but later can be appreciated, and work for your own benefit?

Please meditate on these questions and respond:

- Why would you need to know about the uglies in your life?

- How can you fully initiate positive change without first taking a personal reflection to see what needs changing?
- How can you truly come to the Lord with penance if you see yourself with no faults?

Please read and study in various versions of the bible Proverbs 6:16-19 which depicts the seven deadly sins. Why would it be important for you to know what the Lord hates?

Pride

Do you know anyone who is prideful? Do they appear to believe they are entitled or superior?

Have you ever felt you were better than other people?

Please read and study 1 John 2:16. What are the three main temptations we face?

Have you ever said or thought something like the following sentence? Did you have an attitude of pride? In essence, were you taking all the credit for accomplishments in life?

"Look what I have done all by myself; I am self-made and self-sufficient. Look at me!"

What is the opposite of a prideful heart? How does the Lord view a humble and grateful heart?

Please read and study passages that address pride, humility, and gratitude.

Is there any consequence for people who are prideful? What happened to King Uzziah in 2 Chronicles 26? What happened to Herod in Acts 12?

Please read and study the parable of the Pharisee and the tax collector in Luke 18. What does Jesus say about pride?

Is there a remedy when you realize you have been prideful? Remember Hezekiah in 2 Chronicles 32:25-26. At first Hezekiah was proud and experienced consequences; but he repented of his pride, and God relented.

Greed

Do you know anyone who is greedy? Are they ever satisfied? Will they step on you or others to get what they want?

Have you seen greed in yourself? What can you do about it?

What does the phrase "the love of money is the root of all kinds of evil" mean to you? If a person loves money, then does it become the object or idol of their greed?

Do you agree that our earthly treasures are in stages of decay and when we die, they are left behind?

Lust

Do you know anyone whose mind appears to be fixed on specific desires? Do you find their lustful ways excessive or offensive?

Have you ever desired something to excess? Did your focus become a problem, such as an addiction or compulsion?

Have you or other people you know found out the hard way that there are a multitude of potential consequences or unwanted results when a person is successful in triggering lust?

Please read and study Proverbs 5:3-22, an interesting story relating to seduction. Were you able to find wisdom in this cautionary tale?

What is the secret to contentment that King David spoke of in Psalm 63:5-8?

Envy

Have you ever been envious of what another person had? Did you feel you should have been the one to have what they had?

How do you feel when you are envious or jealous of what someone else has? Does resentment and dissatisfaction follow envy?

What are some good choices to make instead of fueling envy?

Have you ever overshared? Were you so happy in the moment with the blessing you received that you failed to think about how your news may adversely affect your audience? How can you do better in the future?

Gluttony

When you hear the word 'gluttony,' what do you envision? It is not all about a person being overweight! How do you see gluttony play in with greed and pride?

Are there areas where you are making choices that bring on problems with your health? Is there something you can do about it? What is the first step in the recipe to overcome?

Wrath

Have you ever reacted to a situation to the point of extreme anger, rage, or indignation?Please meditate on the following passage of Ephesians 4:26-27 and look it up in several versions. What do you understand from this?

> But don't let the passion of your emotions lead you to sin!
> Don't let anger control you *or be fuel for revenge*, not for even a day.
> Don't give the slanderous accuser, the Devil, an opportunity to manipulate you!
>
> Ephesians 4:26-27 (TPT) The Passion Translation

Sloth

Do you know anyone who believes they are too good to perform certain jobs or acts of labor? In that attitude, are they being prideful or thinking themselves as entitled to more than others?

What did Jesus do when He came to earth? He served the Heavenly Father, and He served people. Jesus, who was the only begotten Son of God chose not to think of Himself as better than other people. What does that tell you about ideas of entitlement?

Have you ever felt like doing nothing? What does the following scripture bring to light?

Taking the easy way out is the habit of a lazy man, and it will be his downfall.
All day long he thinks about all the things that he craves,for he hasn't learned the secret that the generous man has learned: extravagant giving never leads to poverty.

Proverbs 21:25-26 (TPT) The Passion Translation

Please meditate on the following scripture and share what it speaks to you.

Stop loving this evil world and all that it offers you, for when you love these things you show that you do not really love God; for all these worldly things, these evil desires—the craze for sex, the ambition to buy everything that appeals to you, and the pride that comes from wealth and importance—these are not from God. They are from this evil world itself.
And this world is fading away, and these evil, forbidden things will go with it,
but whoever keeps doing the will of God will live forever.
1 John 2:15-17 (TLB) The Living Bible

Affirmation Statement:

Write an affirmation, with a corresponding scripture or reference.

Gratitude Statement:

Write something you are grateful to the Lord for (recommended daily).

8

HAVE YOU BEEN MALICIOUS INSIDE?

In this chapter, we take a closer look at anger and rage that may reach to evil or malicious thoughts, feelings or intentions that are inside of us.

Have you ever been angry to the point that you felt rage within you? Did it reach the point of hatred toward another person? What did you do about it?

Have you or your loved ones survived injustice? Did it leave you with feelings of wrath? Did you have fantasies of revenge?

Looking back, do you see an instance in your life that you were malicious inside, such as road rage? Did you act upon it verbally or physically?

Please meditate on the following scripture. The world may tell you to get revenge, while religions may condemn you if you get angry at all. What is your understanding that the Apostle Paul is advising?

Go ahead and be angry. You do well to be angry—but don't use your anger as fuel for revenge. And don't stay angry.
Don't go to bed angry.
Don't give the Devil that kind of foothold in your life.
Ephesians 4:26-27 (MSG) The Message

Please read and study Proverbs 4:23-27. What does "leave evil in the dust" mean to you?

What can you do to prevent a negative reaction when others have mistreated or offended you?

Through self-awareness before the offenses come, you are better equipped to handle offenses with a slow response instead of a quick, emotional reaction. Please write your impressions to these affirmative statements:

- Prayerfully I can be aware of my weakness and lean on the Lord.
- I know the enemy is a liar.
- I accepted Jesus and have confidence that I am a loved child of God.
- In times of trouble, I depend immeditately upon God's strength.

Are you authentic with yourself? Do you outwardly respond well to offenses, but smolder inside? What can you do? (hint: refer to the recipe to overcome)

Jesus said that if we have adultery in our heart and mind, then we've committed it already (Matthew 5:28). But don't we tend to try to fool ourselves into thinking there is a vast grey area between right and wrong? Consider these choices:

- If we entertain thoughts of revenge but do not carry them out, are we still mean-spirited?

- What if we plot and plan an offense, but abandon the idea, and instead repent of it?

- What if we had thought about retaliating by harming that adversary physically, but instead gossip to ruin their reputation- is that less mean-spirited?

Please read and study Proverbs 23:7 and Luke 6:45. Please write down your opinion regarding the following statement: "Crimes begin with free-flowing vengeful, poisonous thoughts."

Ask yourself (without considering any reasons or excuses) if you have acted maliciously toward another person. Do you agree that there is no lasting satisfaction in evilness (such as saying or doing harm to another person)?

When we are convicted of malicious thoughts, words, or actions, what can we do? What is the remedy?

Please describe a time when you have done this: With a humble, contrite heart, you turned to God for forgiveness and walked away from that maliciousness. How did you feel after that weight had been lifted from you?

Please pray and meditate on the following scripture. Did any of these seven things bring conviction to your heart for repentance?

These six *things* the LORD hates,
Yes, seven *are* an abomination to Him: A proud look,
A lying tongue,
Hands that shed innocent blood, A heart that devises wicked plans,
Feet that are swift in running to evil,
A false witness *who* speaks lies,
And one who sows discord among brethren.
Proverbs 6:16-19 (NKJV) New King James Version

What are your thoughts regarding the following sentence:
Not every person who screamed, "Crucify Him!" took actual part in crucifying Jesus Christ, but they were still just as guilty of shedding His innocent blood because they were malicious and murderous in their heart.

Does this comment bring you to rethink your stand with controversial matters?

Please keep in mind: We will find many evil things to tempt us because of convenience for ourselves; we can always find a rationale to support whatever choices we make; and often the law of the land will not reflect a moral marker.

In Deuteronomy 30:19, we're encouraged to choose life. We have free will to make choices daily! Are there any choices you have made that you now feel conviction about? Can you turn to God about it right now?

Please read and study 1 Peter 5:8. What habits, compulsions, or addictions may hinder the soundness of our decisions? Please comment on the following statement:

As much as we can control ourselves in making sound decisions, it is good to do so; while we maintain a sound mind, we can avoid a multitude of mistakes.

How might knowledge of statistics in relation to the propensity to make certain mistakes become helpful to you?

Have you fallen victim to a malicious person's words or actions? Please read and study Psalm 27:11-14 and Psalm 28:6-7. Were they helpful?

Do you know that you can always run to your Heavenly Father to deliver you from troubles?

Affirmation Statement:

Write an affirmation, with a corresponding scripture or reference.

Gratitude Statement:

Write something you are grateful to the Lord for (recommended daily).

9

ARE YOU EXPERIENCING SPIRITUAL WARFARE?

In this chapter, we address spiritual warfare (good and evil) that is happening all around us.

Do you believe that both God and His angels (good) and the devil with his army (evil) exist and are battling for our soul?

Please read and study Ephesians 6 and this chapter, then briefly write down each piece of the armor of God with corresponding specific purpose (scant outline is listed for help).

Helmet

Breastplate

Belt

Shoes

Shield

Sword

Prayer

Cloak

Can you give an example of when and how you have sensed that this spiritual battle was happening?

While you were in that battle (your previously listed example), did you know what to do? Were you helpless to what may happen next?

Did you know that the name of Jesus is powerful? When you cry out to Jesus, do you believe He will hear you and rescue you, as He promises to do in the Word of God?

From reading and studying Ephesians 6 and this chapter, do you better understand what to do to prepare for when the enemy attacks?

As we noted in Daniel 10, there may be a waiting period between your cry out to the Lord for help and when rescue comes. Did you realize that during that wait-time the Lord's angels may be in battle with the enemies of darkness? How might patient faith strengthen your resolve while you wait?

The enemy's fiery darts or flaming arrows may come in the form of evil whispers, suggestions, and temptations. Have you experienced it? Were you helpless in it, or did you turn to the Lord?

Are you a believer in Jesus Christ? How has He prepared and equipped you to hold your thoughts captive? What does that mean? (hint: please read and study 2 Corinthians 10:5; Romans 12:2; and James 4:7)

How effectively can your shield deflect the enemy's attacks if your faith falters?

Which piece of the Armor is your weapon? Please read and study the following passage:

> Every Scripture has been written by the Holy Spirit,
> the breath of God.
> It will empower you by its instruction and correction, giving you
> the strength to take the right direction and lead you
> deeper into the path of godliness.
> 2 Timothy 3:16 (TPT) The Passion Translation

With the Word of God as your weapon against the enemy attacks, how important is it then, that you saturate yourself with the Word of God?

How can you be prepared for battle and have your weapon drawn? Can you regularly get into the Word of God, pray, and praise the Lord? Can you memorize favorite passages that speak to you? Can you create daily affirmations from your favorite scriptures or set them to a tune for singing?

In what ways can you wield your weapon while you are under the enemy attacks? (hint: refer to the previous questions)

Please read and study Joshua 1:7-9. Are you to face battle alone while in fear? Who promises to be with you wherever you go?

Please write down how you can utilize these following elements of your full armor of God.

- Bind yourself with truth;
- Wear the righteousness of Jesus;
- Be well grounded with thanksgiving;
- Demonstrate the peace of God as your anchor;
- Have faith;
- Wear your helmet of salvation; and
- Know and utilize the Word of God.

How did you fare with the Pandemic? Were you well able to wear your armor? Which prevailed, your fear or your faith? What did you learn from that experience? Do you believe that you will be better able to face the next enemy attack or circumstance with your full armor on?

As I wrote *A New Song Rises Up*, I faced challenges. Some challenges were small, but others were huge; namely, the Pandemic, my son's sudden death, and my PTSD (post-traumatic stress disorder) flashback experiences. What have you experienced within the past six months?

Enemy attacks are real! Can you agree with the following statement?

"For such a time as this, it is before our trials, tribulations, or circumstances happen that we must ensure our full armor is in place, ensure we have our weapon drawn and ready for what we may face."

If you are a believer of Jesus Christ, you are not alone; the Holy Spirit is with you. What does the Holy Spirit do?

Please read and study Galatians 5:22-23. What does the Holy Spirit equip us with? How do we develop this fruit of the Spirit that's given to us?

Please read and study the greatest commandment, found in Matthew 22:37-40. Please write it down here:

Please read and study the Parable of the Good Samaritan, found in

Luke 10:25-37. Who is your neighbor?

Please read and study the great commission, found in Matthew 28:19-20. What actions are believers of Jesus Christ instructed to do?

Please read and study Romans 12, Ephesians 4, and 1 Corinthians 12 regarding Spiritual Gifts. What does the Holy Spirit empower every follower of Jesus Christ with?

Do you have an idea of what your specific Spiritual Gifts might be? Maybe some gifts are only for a season of time? You can ask the Lord about it and wait for His answer. Meanwhile, this would be a great topic to console with your Pastor about and study.

As a result of your study while in this chapter, please name some of the things that the Lord has provided for each of us so we can stand when the enemy attacks.

Affirmation Statement:

Write an affirmation, with a corresponding scripture or reference.

Gratitude Statement:

Write something you are grateful to the Lord for (recommended daily).

10

WERE YOU OPPRESSED?

In this chapter, we discuss the effects of abuse a victim has endured, and the on-going and overwhelming burden that results from the cruel power over them.

Have you had to endure such oppression? Have you broken free from the effects of it?

Did you experience abuse? There are many types of abuse (for more information on types of abuse, refer to *www. CarinJayneCasey.com* and to *My Dear Rosa Jean*), but in this chapter we looked at three that relate to my testimony of receiving a tattoo against my will. Please indicate how each of these types of abuse tie in with that story:

Psychological

Emotional

Physical

Can you relate to the desperation felt by a victim with scarring or other unwanted markings on their body?

From this story, what did you come to understand about a typical abuser?

- Was the abuser in control of the situation?
- Had the abuser exercised planning?
- Did the abuser manipulate the victim's boundaries or moral compass?
- Was there a series of affronts designed to cause the victim fear, anxiety, and confusion?
- Was the goal to cause lasting physical, emotional, and psychological harm?
- Did the abuser attempt to influence their victim's plight as hopeless?

What type of negative feelings would a victim have as result of this kind of assault?

How might such a victim view themselves during and after their experience with an abuser?

The incident described in the story happened decades ago, and there is better help available for victims of domestic violence today. Do you know the National Domestic Violence Hotline number? 1-800-799-7233

Do you know shelter reference numbers for your local area?

What are some things that a victim of abuse can do toward recovery? (hint: refer to the recipe to overcome)

What does the Serenity Prayer say? What would you decide to do if faced with such a situation?

Have you found yourself judging or criticizing any particular group of people? Knowing that the Lord says, "Judge not, lest ye be judged!" Can you repent?

Do you know who you are in Christ Jesus? How will knowing who you are in Him strengthen your resolve when you find yourself down, but not destroyed?

Can you remember a time when you were approaching the depth of a dark pit, and the Lord had scooped you out of your troubles? Can you remember the love, mercy, and compassion He showed you for future enemy attacks?

Do you believe that Jesus knows exactly how it feels to be hurt, rejected, abused, betrayed, lied to and about, and shamed? Do you believe He is right there with you when you believe and accept Him as your Lord and Savior?

Do you know what your weaknesses are? Can you look at past incidents as learning tools?

- Can you learn obedience and reliance upon the Lord?
- Can you learn empathy toward others who may suffer with the same weakness?
- Can you use the instance as an opportunity to mature along your walk?
- Can you be prepared for the future with your armor of God on (as in Ephesians 6)?

Please read and study Romans 8:28. Do you love the Lord? Do you believe that while the enemy seeks to harm you, that the Lord can work that situation ultimately for your good?

Affirmation Statement:

Write an affirmation, with a corresponding scripture or reference.

Gratitude Statement:

Write something you are grateful to the Lord for (recommended daily).

11

WILL YOU REAP WHAT YOU SOW?

In this chapter, we address sowing and reaping, which are the choices we make, and the corresponding results, based upon our decisions. When we sow or plant good seeds, we can hope for a harvest, answered prayers, or rewards. But when we plant bad seeds, we face consequences.

Please read and study Matthew 13:1-23, Mark 4:1-20, and Luke 8:4-15. What did you understand about sowing and reaping from these Parables?

With the narrative presented to you, were you better able to understand the concept of heaven and hell, and the role that Jesus' crucifixion and resurrection plays in the hereafter?

Have you turned to God for forgiveness? Do you believe Jesus is the Son of God, who died on the cross to pay for your sins, and arose from the grave? Do you accept Jesus as your Lord and Savior? If yes, then you are a believer, saved, born again.

If you are saved by the blood of Jesus, how long are you saved?

Please read and study Ephesians 2:8-9. After you have accepted Jesus and you are His believer, does your grace through Jesus then depend upon what you do or not do?

In James 1:19 we are advised to be quick to listen, slow to speak, and slow to anger. Have you seen good results from following this advice? Have you seen unpleasant results from failing to do this? Are you lost if you have failed, or can you confess it to the Lord and strive to do better going forward (refer to previous question)?

Have you ever experienced a hardship or trial and learned valuable lessons from it? Were you then able to use that instance to sow seeds or play it forward to help another person?

Have you seen the truth (principle) of a person reaping what they had sown?

- Have you seen a person regret having spread gossip about another person?
- Have you experienced the pain in a broken relationship because of lies that were told?
- Have you witnessed the penalty imposed on someone caught in a theft?
- Have you watched a friend or loved one bring upon themselves consequences?

- Has it happened to you?

If you have done something wrong, maybe a terrible, mean-spirited thing, are you waiting for your consequences? What can you do to ensure right standing with the Lord?

There were a couple of examples in this chapter of people procrastinating their timely correction from wrongdoing. Can you relate to them, either experienced or witnessed in others? Does this encourage you to take action when you receive the gift of conviction?

Please meditate on the following scripture, and list what valuable information you find in it:

Don't be misled—you cannot mock the justice of God. You will always harvest what you plant. Those who live only to satisfy their own sinful nature will harvest decay and death from that sinful nature. But those who live to please the Spirit will harvest everlasting life from the Spirit. So let's not get tired of doing what is good. At just the right time we will reap a harvest of blessing if we don't give up. Therefore, whenever we have the opportunity, we should do good to everyone— especially to those in the family of faith. Galatians 6:7-10 (NLT) New Living Translation

In Galatians 6:9, we are encouraged to sow good seed and we will reap a harvest if we don't lose heart or if we don't give up. Have you experienced this in your life that you have had patient faith while you wait for your harvest, reward, or answered prayer?

Was it encouraging to read that others have had to wait a very long time to reach their harvest or to see the good that comes from their sowing good seeds?

What if you sow seeds and reach one specific person with the good news of Jesus, and that one person is instrumental as a great vessel to open doors for many people to come to God's Kingdom? How awesome would that be?

Did you take on a project that would be helpful to others, but then you became busy, distracted, bored, discouraged, or lose interest? Sometimes we start with a generous intent, but life gets in the way. Can you prayerfully keep yourself motivated and not quit?

Please read and study Matthew 6:1. Have you received unanticipated rewards while in efforts to do good? Were you swayed by the attention and accolades? Were you able to maintain your focus on the purpose of those efforts?

Do you agree that as you sow gratefulness, you will reap a harvest of blessings?

Affirmation Statement:

Write an affirmation, with a corresponding scripture or reference.

Gratitude Statement:

Write something you are grateful to the Lord for (recommended daily).

12

DID YOU COME TO JESUS?

This is such an important question! As you read my journey, please think about your relationship with Jesus. Have you made that important decision?

On that significant Sunday morning, do you believe the Lord was leading me to Him? Have you felt the Lord leading you? How did you respond?

In my story, I shared that I sang with the others so they would not realize I was not a believer. Have you been pretending so that others would not pressure you? If so, I urge you to face it and be authentic with yourself, and with Jesus.

Have you ever felt as if there was spiritual presence, whether whispers or reminders of good and lovely things, or of wicked, evil things? How were you influenced?

What is your response to the following questions? "Does it make sense to refuse the only way, the truth and the life? To give up eternity because of the choices other people (who were toxic or abusive) had made?"

We know bad stuff will happen on earth and sometimes we do not understand. What is your response to the following dialog?

The enemy whispered, "What God would allow the pain and suffering of innocent children? Where was God when terrible things happened to you?"

Then Jesus said, "I was with you through it all! And I am with you now! I will never leave you! Suffering on earth is only for a moment compared to the joy of everlasting life with Me!"

Have you accepted Jesus as your Lord and Savior, and you were intensely focused on the Lord for several years and enjoyed inner peace and joy; but over time, did you begin to allow life's distractions to affect you?

Did you know that God knew you would have distractions? The enemy wants you to believe you have lost your place in the Kingdom of God, but you have not. Respectfully, with a humble contrite heart, come to Jesus about it. Do you need to come to Jesus about anything you are remorseful or feel convicted about now?

Why did the Lord forgive you? Why did He forgive King David when he caused the death of a man to cover his adultery? Why did He forgive Saul, who persecuted Christians before God showed him the truth? Why did He forgive me? Do you believe that the Lord is all-knowing? Merciful? That God *is* love?

Have you come to a point to rededicate your life to Jesus? He had never left you from the day you accepted Jesus as your Lord and Savior. Whether you remained a Baby Christian five years or a decade, His unfailing patience remained. Do you believe it?

If you are not yet a believer, can you now decide to humbly turn to Him while you have the opportunity? If you are ready, please repeat out loud my version of what is frequently referred as the sinner's prayer that follows (which always contains key elements from the word of God):

"Dear Lord Jesus,
I know that You are the only begotten Son of God.
I know that You suffered on the cross for me, for my sins.
And I believe that You defeated death.
You arose from the grave on the third day.
But, I'm a sinner! I ask You to forgive me.
I repent of my sins. I walk away from them now.
Please help me stand firm, because I know I will be tempted.
I need You, Jesus!
I am nothing, I am hopeless without You.
I ask You, Jesus, to come into my heart and to be my Lord and Savior.
And I will serve You all of my life!
In Jesus Name,
Amen."

If you have sincerely said this prayer to the Lord, then you belong to Jesus. Please write down in your own words what it means to you to know that you are a believer (also called born again, saved, a Child of God).

Once redeemed, you are a new creature and the Holy Spirit dwells in you. What change has happened? Are you ever alone?

Not all at once, but you will grow in your faith. Please read and study Galatians 5:22-23. What has the Holy Spirit equipped you with?

Please read and study Philippians 2:12-13 and describe what it means to you to walk out or work out your salvation.

What are some of the things you plan to do in your quest to grow and mature in your Christian walk?

What is your response to these statements:
"When you follow Jesus, you are the light of the world! The Holy Spirit within you will motivate you to encourage and help others, so your light will shine.".

Affirmation Statement:

Write an affirmation, with a corresponding scripture or reference.

Gratitude Statement:

Write something you are grateful to the Lord for (recommended daily).

13

CAN YOU RUN THE RACE?

In this chapter, we explore the quest of a Christian to realize their purpose in life, and to pursue that path.

Is there something that you keep in your heart and mind, maybe a dream, talent, or goal, that you believe you should be doing in life? Do you know what your purpose in life is? Are you asking God about it?

Have you been discouraged from taking that first step toward your dream? Were you filled with fear? Can you prayerfully take any lack of faith to the Lord, and re-start?

Do you believe that the Lord prepares you for your purpose in life? Please read and study Jeremiah 1:5 and Jeremiah 29:11, and state what they tell you.

Can you feel the conflict between God's good plan for your life versus the enemy working to harm you? What does Ephesians 6 and John 10:10 tell you about this spiritual battle?

As you face challenges in life, can you say the following scripture with your resolve?

> But me, I'm not giving up.
> I'm sticking around to see what GOD will do.
> I'm waiting for God to make things right. I'm counting on
> God to listen to me.
> Don't, enemy, crow over me. I'm down, but I'm not out.
> I'm sitting in the dark right now, but GOD is my light.
> Micah 7:7-8 (MSG) The Message

What are some things you can plan to do for when you are tempted to give up on what you believe you were meant to do? What can you do to make sure you remain zealous and not mediocre in what you know you have been called to do?

Please read and study Jeremiah 17:7-8 and Genesis 50:20 and respond to the following sentence: "Please remember, what the enemy has meant for your harm, God will make for your good, so you can fulfill the unique purpose He put in you."

Please read Daniel 3:17-18, the story about Shadrach, Meshach, and Abednego. Can you prayerfully and confidently say, "My God will deliver me from this circumstance; But if not, I will still worship Him." Would your mind be focused on Eternity, rather than earth?

The Apostle Paul gave the secret to having an attitude of contentment in 2 Corinthians 4:17-18. Can you give an example in your life where this can be applied?

In your specific purpose, what does it look like to press on?

Please comment on these statements:

- "In all we do, we can take a stand for the Lord and His commandments.".
- "We can run that race with unfailing faith in God, even when heartbreaking losses happen.".
- "We can be obedient during our mourning, even while not understanding why things happened the way they did.".
- "We can press on with self-discipline, as described in 1 Corinthians 9:24-27."

Please meditate on the following scripture and decide whether you can be strong and courageous in an uncertain future:

> Have I not commanded you? Be strong and courageous.
> Do not be afraid; do not be discouraged,
> for the LORD your God will be with you wherever you go.
> Joshua 1:9 (NIV) New International Version

Do you know what the Lord's plan for your life is? What will it take to accomplish what God has equipped you to do?

If you do not know what your purpose in life is, can you prayerfully ask the Lord to give you dreams, desires, and guidance within that unique purpose?

Please read and study Philippians 3:13-14. What does it mean to you to press on and to run your race? Can you make a regular affirmation toward that goal to encourage yourself daily?

When the Lord prompts you with your specific calling, will you say "Yes," and begin your journey, one step of faith at a time?

- When in your race, will you give it your all?
- Do you anticipate there will be periods that the race requires courage and hard work, but you have decided to press on?
- Are you determined to maintain your hope and prayerful, patient faith through to the end, knowing that you are not alone in it?

Affirmation Statement:

Write an affirmation, with a corresponding scripture or reference.

Gratitude Statement:

Write something you are grateful to the Lord for (recommended daily).

14

EPILOGUE

In the Epilogue, we attempt to summarize and highlight some crucial points found throughout *A New Song Rises Up!*

Please read and study Psalm 107:23-32. Were you able to resonate with being caught within a terrible storm in life, calling out to the Lord for deliverance and redemption, with the Lord lifting you up?

Did *A New Song Rises Up!* bring you encouragement for when you face your hardships? Were you influenced to turn to the Lord?

Through my testimony of the Lord causing an overcoming from traumatic periods in life, were you able to see how loving and merciful our God is?

Please describe a dark circumstance in your life where God has proven that He is loving and merciful.

Do you believe you have experienced maturity through challenges?

Would you like to give your testimony to others of how great God is because He delivered you?

Do you believe that regardless of what harm the enemy brings you, the Lord had a good plan for you? Please share your examples.

Please state, in your own words, details to the following steps and say whether you have successfully taken these steps. Please describe what actions you can take, in every instance when you face various trials or adversity?

Turn to God

Safely Leave Your Dangerous Environment

Believe and Have Faith

Be Filled with Gratitude

Forgive Yourself, Those Who Abused or Offended You, and the Indifferent

Which of these steps was the most difficult for you? Why was that step the most difficult?

Please meditate on the following scriptures. What do they mean to you? Does your gratitude toward the Lord motivate you to share with others how awesome He is? In what ways has He brought redemption and transformation into your life?

Sing a new song to the LORD!...
Psalm 96:1 (NLT) New Living Translation (portion)

He has given me a new song to sing, a hymn of praise to our God.
Psalm 40:1-3 (NLT) New Living Translation (portion)

Affirmation Statement:

Write an affirmation, with a corresponding scripture or reference.

Gratitude Statement:

Write something you are grateful to the Lord for (recommended daily).

A SHORT NOTE

Dear Precious Readers,

Was this Study Guide helpful? Did my questions and passages encourage you to expand your understanding?

If you were influenced or encouraged in any way, please let me know! I am always eager to receive your comments, suggestions, or any feedback you may be willing to share.

You can reach out to me through my website:

https://www.CarinJayneCasey.com

Thank you, and I pray for your many blessings over you and your loved ones' lives.

In Christ,

Carin

ABOUT THE AUTHOR

Carin Jayne Casey, the oldest of several children, grew up in a dysfunctional, sometimes violent home. Her family had moved from Ohio to rural West Virginia while she was a teen when tragedy struck their family. Casey married her high-school sweetheart and bore two wonderful children. Her marriage failed, and she was eventually lured into a violent and life-threatening relationship.

Casey is an author, speaker, domestic violence advocate and an ambassador for Christ. She strives to educate and encourage people to conquer life challenges. As she recovered from domestic violence, her gratitude toward the Lord motivated her to write books and to provide podcasts for others to gain tools in their overcoming process, to find victory and enjoy life.

Casey served four years on the Board of Directors for Yeshua's House (www.yeshuashouse.net), a faith-based, non-profit safe haven for women overcoming domestic violence and/or financial issues. She currently participates in various outreach and mission efforts with local church groups.

Casey graduated from Radford University and served the Commonwealth of Virginia for 31 years. Carin Jayne Casey is the author's pen name.

Author. Speaker. Podcaster. Advocate. Ambassador.
www.CarinJayneCasey.com
www.Facebook.com/Turn2GodwCarin
CarinJayneCasey - @Turn2GodwCarin on Instagram

ALSO BY CARIN JAYNE CASEY

Carin Jayne Casey has written several books:

- *My Dear Rosa Jean:* Suspense, Fiction, Christian fiction; It depicts a woman's process of overcoming domestic violence and finding victory.

- *Mystery at Candice Bay:* Mystery, Fiction, Young Adult; This is a page-turner, involving teens and their community experiencing escalating alarm as they are bombarded with unexplained events.

- *Granny Babysits the Mischievous Five:* Children's Chapter Book.

Casey continues as a podcaster since 2016 with a weekly podcast, *Turn to God with Carin* to promote hope in healing and overcoming challenges. All her videos are available at Carin Jayne Casey on YouTube.

CPSIA information can be obtained
at www.ICGtesting.com
Printed in the USA
LVHW040139091020
668359LV00015B/946